Marcha

The
Executive Secretary
Guide to
Building a Successful
Career Strategy

Julia Schmidt

Marcham Publishing

Cover image by missimoinsane
http://missimoinsane.deviantart.com/

For Ranulfo, Ir. Graça, and João Batista.
Thousands of miles away but always in my thoughts.

Foreword
by Bonnie Low-Kramen

Julia Schmidt and I first met in London in 2014 sitting across from one another at dinner at Executive Secretary LIVE. I distinctly remember her quiet confidence, commanding presence, and most of all, her insights. As this American got to know this Brazilian/Norwegian, I quickly learned that Julia was a professional who had a lot to say, which is why I am delighted and honored to write the foreword for her first book.

And what an impressive and audacious book it is! Imagine that Julia is actually presenting the radical notion that assistants should not wait for permission to build a career strategy. She not only makes the case for it, but does it brilliantly.

Julia advocates a significant change of mindset for the world's assistants from a minor support player in the workplace to a leader who functions as an executive business partner. This is no small shift for the 250 million assistants in the world.

Julia asks some very tough questions like: What are you here for? and What is your legacy? The answers to these questions are just the beginning of learning how to take control of your career and your life. She urges us to be the CEO of ourselves and I could not agree more. There is no better time to take charge of our life than right now.

The heart of the matter is that you can't be it if you can't see it. Julia shows us the way through her research and through her hard-earned journey to her dream job. I love that she has walked her talk and in pulling back the curtain on her experience, we can all do it too.

If you have been searching for a roadmap for what's next in your career, read this book carefully.

Bonnie Low-Kramen
Best-selling Author, Be the Ultimate Assistant. Speaker. Workplace Activist.

Contents

Introduction

As Executive Assistants, we are daily juggling multiple roles, managing people, delivering under pressure, solving problems and allowing our executives to focus on the core business. Very often, due to all our daily work obligations, we do not allow ourselves time to see the big picture and ask ourselves how we can be strategic in getting what we want. Being strategic means taking the necessary steps to go further in our profession, to become better than we are today and to gain new victories.

I wanted to write a book to really help Assistants understand the need for purpose, ownership, collaboration, alignment, and execution to succeed in the workplace. All this is achievable by having a clear strategic plan to help you attain your goals and become a better version of yourself. I wanted to explore the theories about strategic planning and how they can help us apply the theory in building our career strategy. This book is all about building YOUR career strategy.

Business strategy is all about choices. You must have a clear choice of WHO you are going to serve, and a clear choice of HOW you are going to serve those clients. My view is that as Executive Assistants, we serve our managers and executives (our direct clients) and consequently all of the company's external customers. In addition, we are serving ourselves. We give meaning to our careers and lives through work.

At the end of the day, if you do not think about a strategy that will guarantee you a place in the future of work, then your career will have no future. The skills needed in the labour market change quickly. Therefore, it is crucial that each one of us engages in life-long learning to achieve fulfilling and rewarding careers. It is not merely about remaining employable but also about maximizing our employment opportunities.

People say that life is short. The time to create a successful career is even shorter. Work and career are significant elements in life. Creating a life that matters encompasses a range of factors — physical, emotional, financial, social, career, community, environmental, creative, and even spiritual dimensions.

Who is this book for?

This book is for you, if you believe in the importance of planning your career together with your manager or executive. This book is about creating alliances that will minimize the gap between organization strategy and your career strategy.

Experts in strategy planning know that one of the most critical tactics in building a culture of accountability around the most important strategic questions is to involve a larger part of the organization in a discussion on how the company is doing on strategy and execution. So, my understanding is that every Executive Assistant should do the same regarding her or his professional development. Are all employees involved in the strategic planning? Yes! Is your team of executives involved in your career strategy planning? Yes, of course! We need to involve our executives and managers in the process of building our career strategy. By doing that we will create win-win situations. It is all about aligning the big picture with the employee's day-to-day tasks, and effectively being able to connect individual work to the strategy of the organization.

What we put in our work performance, every single day, is a result of what we have accumulated in terms of expertise, skills, and years of personal and professional experience.

This book is for you, if you want to become the CEO of your career, and simultaneously be a co-leader in helping your organization attain its strategic goals. You are part of the game and it is not a solo game.

Are you a millennial? A Gallup report "How Millennials Want to Work and Live" reveals that millennial career happiness is down, while disengagement at work is climbing. So, make your involvement in the strategy planning a source of job satisfaction. As many as 71% of millennials are not engaged on the job and half of all employees plan on leaving within a year. "Millennials don't just work for a paycheck – they want a purpose." "Millennials are not pursuing job satisfaction – they are pursuing development."

Do you think that only millennials are seeking career development and job satisfaction? The answer is "No." During the last few years, this "millennials' way of being" has become a general rule for many professionals. Most "non-millennials" are also driven by purpose and development. We are learning it from colleagues, friends and millennial leaders. In reality, we are all hungry for feedback, appraisals, and professional growth.

A call to action

I want this book to be a call to action. I want you to understand that you shall not let the bosses keep carrying the responsibility alone for our job disengagement. I want you to become the CEO of your career, to take responsibility for creating opportunities for growth and learning, involving your managers in your career journey, and aligning your career strategy with your company's strategy. This is what I have learned in the last fifteen years and will be sharing with you in the coming chapters.

It takes time to plan your career and you need to understand that you have to invest time in that process. Also, you must remember that planning needs consistency and active engagement. If you have big goals and great dreams, you have to find out how to accomplish them. This is what I want to offer you with this book: the opportunity to sit down, evaluate your needs, look at all alternatives, assess your skills set, re-discover your dreams, define your priorities, and start planning for the future of work. If you have the predictable things under control, you will be able to manage the disruptive ones with more confidence.

I want you to go through several self-assessment exercises. Use this book to discover and define what drives you professionally, find out if you are on the right path, expand your career goals, create your purpose and vision and provide yourself with appropriate challenges. Take a pen, some post-its and a small notebook that you can easily carry with you. Get inspired by the career development conversation you are going to have with yourself, and that will allow you to build a successful career strategy.

Before we start

I have some tips for you that will help you get the most out of this book:

- Schedule time to read the book;

- Take time to answer the questions;

- Write down any ideas that may occur to you while reading;

- Be open, direct and honest with yourself;

- Share with others what you will be learning;

- Value your strengths and acknowledge your weaknesses;

- Be willing to step outside your comfort zone;

- Create your own career strategy tool-kit;

- Take the lead;

- Hold yourself accountable for your career strategy;

- Be ready for new win-win situations.

Building a successful career strategy

My model is based on five steps that are directly related to how business strategy planning is normally created and executed. The book is broken down into six chapters.

The first chapter sets the stage to help us understand WHY strategic thinking is more relevant than ever. The second presents a guideline on how to define your purpose and make it the fuel that will release the energy you need to keep your strategy in motion. Chapters three to five explore the vital elements in any strategic planning – alignment, execution and how we can make success happen. The last chapter provides some inspirational quotes on strategy execution. They will keep us inspired on the way and remind us that commitment and high performance are the keys to success.

Let's start our journey. Take a comfortable seat. Let me introduce you to the five steps to building a successful career strategy by combining personal and professional goals, and the six chapters that I hope will inspire you to build a better future for your life.

The five-step model

The six chapters

Chapter One: Knowing the Why
Chapter Two: Creating Purpose
Chapter Three: Aligning the Goals
Chapter Four: Executing the Actions
Chapter Five: Achieving Success
Chapter Six: Inspirational Quotes on Strategy Execution

For those of you who want to connect with me directly, you can do so by:

emailing me at Julia_Schmidt@hotmail.com,

connecting with me on twitter at @Julia_SchmidtEA

or via LinkedIn:
https://www.linkedin.com/in/juliaschmidtea/

I look forward to hearing from you!

1

Knowing the Why

There is nothing like a dream to create the future.
– Victor Hugo

Why a Strategy?

The word 'strategy' is defined as a method or plan chosen to bring about a desired future, such as the achievement of a goal or a solution to a problem. A strategy shall move us from a now situation to a future situation. It is the art and science of planning and marshalling resources for their most efficient and effective use.

We all need a plan in order to keep on growing professionally. The starting point for everything is a strategy. You can have a vision: #BeTheBestAssistant. To get there you have to start with a strategy and an execution plan for that strategy. To build a successful strategy we need to know the Why.

We normally associate the word strategy with the corporate world. We are hearing the word daily in team meetings, board meetings, and strategy workshops and business reviews.

Our companies are defining new strategies to reduce prices of products, to gain new markets, develop new products, retain employees, build a healthier culture, increase customer satisfaction. There are many reasons to develop strategies, and there are other numerous motives for adopting strategies.

The word strategy is then very often associated with change processes. It is all about creating a better future for our business, career, and life.

So why do we need a strategy? Because we need to know the why of what we are doing, follow the right paths to achieve our dreams and goals, understand the importance of our work in the grand scheme of things, structure the tasks we are performing, ensure competitive advantage, keep growing and enhance engagement.

Strategy planning helps us connect the dots. When a strong vision and mission support a dream, managers have the tools they need to develop organizational goals and strategies. This is what creates engagement.

One of the most important things I have learned in being an active contributor in strategy planning in the organizations where I have worked, and in the association for administrative professionals (IMA – International Management Assistants) where I have been board member and Chair of the board, is the enhancement of engagement it creates.

By being involved in different levels, sometimes at the bottom line of the organization and often at the top of the pyramid, I learned that everyone in the organization must contribute, because organizational strategies shall be broken down into team and individual goals, in addition to daily activities. Execution does not happen at the top of the pyramid, it happens when all factors contributing to the big picture are in place, well-articulated and understood by all people involved in the process.

A dream is transformed into vision and mision → The vision and mission create a strategic plan to acheive the dream → The strategic plan generates goals → To acheive the goals, we need daily tasks and activities → The right set of activities leads to the achievement of the dream

This understanding creates engagement, drives execution forces and makes dreams become goals and then reality. This understanding will make alignment possible – your personal goals being aligned with your organization's goals.

Knowing the Why is about being able to view and understand the big picture. The Why will help us think and act strategically. To help us get there, we are going to reflect about eight elements that are crucial in building a strategy. They will help us do a self-assessment. I could have added more elements but wanted to choose the ones that will play an important role in this initial self-assessment (a SWOT analysis). When going through the eight elements, I invite you to reflect, answer the questions, make notes and get into a strategic mindset. Have your pen prepared! The self-assessment will help you analyze:

- Competitive advantage;

- The future of work;

- Skills;

- Risks;

- Market;

- Presence;

- Strengths;

- Professional development.

What is a SWOT analysis (or SWOT matrix)?

It is a strategic planning technique used to help a person or organization identify the *Strengths*, *Weaknesses*,

Opportunities, and *Threats* related to business competition or project planning. It is intended to specify the objectives of the business venture or project and identify the internal and external factors that are favorable and unfavorable to achieving those objectives. Users of a SWOT analysis often ask and answer questions to generate meaningful information for each category to make the tool useful and identify their competitive advantage. (Wikipedia)

A SWOT analysis will help you understand the WHY, because if don't know WHY, you can't know HOW.

Enhancing competitive advantage

We are in a constant pressure to improve productivity, quality and agility. The right strategy will allow us to improve our performance, help us get better results, enhance effectiveness and add extra value to the organization.

Here are some elements that we associate with Business Strategy:

Goals	Ideas	Results	Objectives	Metrics
Review	Process	Target	Improvements	Plan
Action	Execution	Change	Activities	Mission
Vision	Direction	Scope	Long-term	Advantage
Environment	Resources	Competences	Stakeholders	Development

A strategy should be about being unique, rather than being the best. In competitions, there is normally only one winner but in business there can be several winners. It does not have to be a zero-sum game. Strategy is about growth, and to keep growing and moving in today's market, we must sell uniqueness.

Strategy is nothing more than a commitment to a set of coherent, mutually reinforcing policies or behaviours aimed at achieving a specific competitive goal.

Good strategies promote alignment among diverse groups within an organization, clarify objectives and priorities, and help focus efforts around them, says Professor Gary P. Pisano, in the article 'You need an Innovation Strategy' published by Harvard Business Review.

Therefore, as much as organizations need to have a strategy plan, we, as professionals, need to have a career strategy that will allow us to widely contribute to our personal development and consequently to organizational growth.

Aligning your career strategy with your organization's strategy will create numerous win-win situations that will place you on the top of the edge.

We need to remain competitive within our industries, and employers play a significant role in offering their employees opportunities for educational and vocational development that address their needs, to remain relevant and aggressive in pursuing their career goals.

Today's fast-moving digital transformation demands relentless re-innovation, continual reeducation, and constant re-imagination of what's possible both at a personal level and at an organizational level.

Businesses hire knowledge workers to stay in the game. How are you keeping yourself a knowledge worker?

ACTION ITEM

Study each of the elements that are part of a business strategy plan. Use the words listed on the previous graphic.

Understanding the future of work

Non-technological as well as technological structural changes will have major impacts on future skills needs.

Studies show that the future of work is not only influenced by automation and digitization. Many trends are impacting the way we work and the skills in demand: increasing inequality, political uncertainty, technological change, demographic change, globalization, environmental sustainability and urbanization. (The Future of Skills: Employment in 2030 – Executive Summary.)

The reality is that some jobs will be more likely to experience a fall in employment than others. Some industries and services will grow in importance, while others will have to be drastically redefined.

We know that most of studies in this field predict a decline in administrative, secretarial and some sales occupations. This means that we all need to start thinking more strategically towards:

- Building more organizational strategic understanding;

- Analyzing trends;

- Anticipating our participation in the workplace;

- Gaining new skills;

- Targeting new opportunities;

- Creating a board of advisors – people who can and will help you succeed.

Before we find out if we are going in the right direction, we need to understand our current position, by analyzing our strengths, weaknesses, opportunities and threats. This analysis will allow us to define at what level we will be able to actively contribute to the organization's strategy plan and execution. We have to understand the basic professional strengths and weaknesses we have, and the potential opportunities for our development and the likely threats to that development.

ACTION ITEMS

1. Read the studies already published about the future of work.
2. Form a group work to discuss the trends.
3. Read your organization's strategy plan and actions.
4. Read the trends for your industry.
5. Read Mike Kehoe's article – 4 Habits of People Who are Always Learning New Skills:
(https://hbr.org/2018/01/4-habits-of-people-who-are-always-learning-new-skills)

Listing your skills

In the Digital Age, you need to be comfortable with change and you need to be willing to develop new skills.

Bonnie Hagemann, co-author of 'Leading with Vision' and CEO of Executive Development Associates, an executive development consulting firm, says that "the best growth opportunity may be in another role or project and not necessarily moving up." She also says that "sometimes it's stepping down to learn a new skill and then going up again. Think career lattice instead of career ladder."

Do you have the necessary skills? For your employer it is important to have the right resources in the right places. Have you been proactive regarding your development plans? A successful strategy must include appropriate training. Development is an ongoing process. You must avoid the mistake of thinking that you have learned enough. It will never be enough. List the skills you have and the ones you want to acquire. Look for the skills that will:

- make a difference;

- boost your competitive advantage;

- give you competence to help your organization attain its goals;

- keep you employable.

Before you start the exercise, I want to you to understand the definition of skills.

What is the definition of skills?

In the report 'Insight Report Towards a Reskilling Revolution – A Future of Jobs for All', published by the World Economic Forum, I found this definition:

- **Skills** are used to apply knowledge to complete tasks.

- **Cross-functional skills** are skills required by a variety of job roles which are transferable to a broad range of job role.

- **Specialized skills** are particular to an industry or a job role and are not easily transferable (e.g. skills related to the use, design, maintenance and repair of technology).

The list of cross-functional skills I have:

The list of specialized skills I have:

The skills I need (both cross-function and specialized):

Cross-function or specialized	What do I need to do to gain this skill?	Who can help me?

The most valuable skills in the Digital Age

In the introduction of the report 'Robots Need Not Apply', presenting the results of a research carried out in October 2017, Jonas Prising, Chairman and CEO of the Manpower Group says that "in this digital world success will not always require a college degree, but will rely heavily on the appetite for continuous skills development. We must nurture people's curiosity and learnability, so they have the desire and ability to continuously develop their skills to stay employable."

The research also shows that "human strengths are skills that will augment technology and reduce the threat of replacement by automation." It means that we must not underestimate that the complementary use of machines and humans – an optimized combination of human and technological strengths – can be particularly productive.

Here are examples of human skills in demand according to findings from the Manpower Group's research:

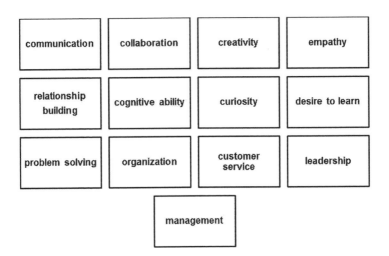

Rate the skills in demand you have on the scale of 1 to 10:

Skills in demand	You are rating yourself	Ask a friend or colleague to rate your skills
Communication		
Collaboration		
Creativity		
Empathy		
Relationship building		
Cognitive ability		
Curiosity		
Desire to learn		
Problem solving		
Organization		
Customer service		
Leadership		
Management		

Once you have completed the table by rating your skills, answer the questions below and create an action plan that will allow you to improve your skills in demand.

Which are the skills in demand that are most valued in my function/role?

Which skills do I have to start improving right now to ensure employability?

Create a short-term plan with concrete strategic actions that will help you improve your skills in demand:

Anticipating risks

New technologies make our day-to-day life different and faster than we realize. Look forward and find what you might be vulnerable to in your career, industry and organization. Be proactive and adaptable. If you see that the Project Coordinator role you have will disappear because a crucial project enters its conclusive phase, do not wait too long to implement a plan B and look for new opportunities. Be innovative and find a new area where you can be a valuable player. Spend time reflecting instead of simply doing. Embrace innovation as your main tool to minimize the risks. Embrace technology and eliminate gaps.

What is risk?

A probability or threat of damage, injury, liability, loss, or any other negative occurrence that is caused by external or internal vulnerabilities, and that may be avoided through pre-emptive action. (Business Dictionary)

List the risks you have already identified and reflect on how you can minimize or eliminate them and who can help you in this task.

What are the risks I have identified?	How can I minimize or eliminate the risks?	Which tools or people do I need to minimize or eliminate the risks?

Understanding your market

Strategy is about knowing where you are going. Your market is represented by the people paying for your services. Your current market is the work environment where you are delivering your service. Remember that being a successful Assistant is about delivering high quality. To be able to play a significant role as a strategist in your organization, you have to feel that you are in the right market. Ask yourself these questions:

How easily could my employer be willing to replace me?

What can I do to keep the current "market" interested in what I am leveraging?

Should I focus on other "markets" (different industry, position or company)?

Are there more attractive "markets" paying better for the services I can deliver or for the skills-set I have?

What can I do to feel comfortable in my "current market"?

We live in a time of extraordinary change. Changes that are shaping the way we live and the way we work. Whether we like it or not, the pace of these changes will only accelerate. If you want to find the right direction and scope of your professional career over the long term and achieve advantage in a world of constant changes, start it now.

Sometimes we are already in the right place. What we forget is to assess our "presence in the market", the value we are already adding and how we can just improve the standard of what we are delivering.

From time to time we will just find out that we have to move on and find something new that will keep boosting our motivation to go to work and make a difference in the workplace.

Valentina, an Office Manager who had worked in the IT industry for many years, had to experience some years working in a different industry to understand that the "right place" for her is in the IT Industry. She told me that she was missing the agile mindset and leaders who are innovative, empower involvement, enable decision making and lead with transparency. Valentina wanted to be part again of collaborative teams.

To adopt any business strategy, we will have to feel that we are in the right place, in the right market.

Ensuring your Presence

Are you appearing strategic in the way you act and communicate with people? Strategic EAs and PAs radiate confidence, use correct words and express opinions with authority. Having a powerful presence by listening to what people are saying and respecting their point of view is a key element of being strategic with a leading presence. Networking is an excellent tool to help us practice a strategic presence. I use networking to improve my listening skills. I listen without judging, get curious rather than judgmental and let people tell their stories.

Being strategic and ensuring your presence in the workplace is directly linked to the kind of "language" you speak. I know that to attain my professional goals I must speak the language of the business. I have to know and understand my organization's strategy, goals, customers, industry and competitors. By attending training courses and industry conferences, reading articles, and following blogs you gain business knowledge.

- Do you speak the business language?

- Are you attending the conferences your executive team attend?

- Are you attending the industry fairs and seminars the managers annually sign up for?

- Are you volunteering for projects?

- Are you speaking as a leader?

I have been very fortunate to have the opportunity to work with great leaders and entrepreneurs. I always learn so much from them. I learn from their leadership styles and collect the best qualities they have. These characteristics go onto my to-be list and as soon as possible, I start practicing the new desired leadership behaviour.

One of the best qualities I have incorporated is the "art of thinking before answering". One of my executives is an excellent listener and always reflect before answering questions. I appreciate every second I have to wait before hearing the calm and reflective answer coming from his mouth. This calm gives so much power to what he says. It also enhances his presence.

ACTION ITEMS

1. Find a relevant industry magazine and subscribe.
2. Read books about leadership and how to act as a leader.
3. Read all industry summaries and reports your managers are reading.
4. Book time for reading in your calendar and explain to your executives why it is important for you to stay updated.
5. Make a notebook for industry words, abbreviations and expressions and memorize the meanings of the most relevant terminologies.

Owning your Strengths

To get where you want, you have to recognize your strengths. Being strategic is about knowing yourself and leveraging the best.

- What are your personal strengths and talents?

- What are you passionate about and how can your passions contribute to a better performance?

- What changes do you need to make to adjust your leadership style?

- Do you need mentors to help you along the way?

If you want to advance professionally you must be able to hold past, present and future in mind at the same time. Start acting! Evaluate your strategic presence, how you have spoken up and played an active role in networking activities in the past twelve months. Study the possibilities you have now, including your strengths, and start being a better strategic thinker. Plan your future today and leverage your power by being determinedly strategic.

The future of our profession is all about technology skills, innovation, flexibility, agility, resilience, continuous learning and human skills.

- Are you prepared for new forms of work?

- Are you working on gaining the necessary skills to keep yourself employable?

Gaining a competitive advantage means growing your competencies. You have certainly heard mentors and coaches mention the importance of creating your Board of Advisors. I personally recommend you create one, in case you do not have it yet. It is crucial to be surrounded by positive people. Your advisors will be a precious source of feedback and feedforward. They are your best collaborators and will keep you on the right path.

There is nothing on the Internet that can replace direct, one-to-one advice from an expert. Therefore, your group of advisors should be composed of knowledgeable individuals having together a set of necessary qualities:

- Being trustworthy, high skilled and successful people;

- Bringing diversity;

- Representing your interests and wanting the best for you and your career;

- Connecting you with the right people and helping you expand your network;

- Giving honest feedback and helping you create and improve your strategic plans;

- Knowing the industry in which you are operating;

- Understanding your profession and goals;

- Having a positive and growth mindset;

- Having time availability.

The members of your Board of Advisors can be your spouse or other family members, colleagues, former manager or executive, current manager, the family doctor, your best friend, teacher or trainer or a successful entrepreneur. They have to help you increase your set of strengths. No matter what you want to do, there are people out there who know how to do it well. You just have to find them and learn from their experiences. Start recruiting your Board of Advisors today! If you already have one, map the qualities they bring to you as a total.

ACTION ITEMS

1 Create your board of advisors and make conversations, interviews and workshops. Surround yourself with people who can help you grow through positive feedback and mentorship.
2 If you already have one, map the qualities they bring to you as a total and find out if there is something missing. How about bringing new people to your board?

Enhancing synergy

One of the best ways to show you own your professional development is by expanding your set of skills and creating synergy.

According to surveys responded to by members of IMA (International Management Assistants) and members' managers, as well as job advertisements and research for the profession, here are the desired skills employers are looking for in Management Support Professionals. The list includes soft skills, that apply to every job. These are people skills – interpersonal skills, communication skills, and other qualities that enable you to be successful in the workplace. The list also has hard skills as for example computer skills, administrative skills, and customer service skills.

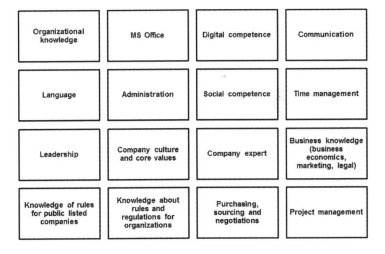

Source: https://www.ima-network.org/profile-management-support-professional

Being your own CEO and investing in your professional development will enable synergy.

I appreciate that many companies are committed to growing competent employees and giving necessary support for professional advancement. Companies are using performance reviews not only to assess an employee's performance, but also to evaluate an employee's future potential. However, my understanding is that each professional has to own her or his career development.

With this in mind, let's embrace a more positive way to look at performance reviews. Let's benefit from this opportunity to align our own career goals with the goals our organization has defined in its strategy plan. Let's build an alliance where we acknowledge that we are working together – executive and executive assistant – to achieve agreed-upon goals. The partnership you build together will bring out the highest potential you have and extend to a higher level – the strategic level.

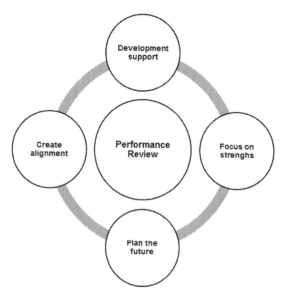

Your career strategy and the organization's strategy should create an interaction resulting in meaningful goals and effective actions for growing the skills needed to help you achieve a successful career by performing at a high-level.

What is synergy?

Synergy is the combined power of a group of things when they are working together that is greater than the total power achieved by each working separately (Cambridge dictionary).

The benefits of synergy are:

- Shared vision, values and goals;

- Strategic actions complementing each other;

- Maximized use of strengths;

- Boosting a collaborative environment.

You should have built a complete analysis of where you are and how do you want to strengthen your positioning in the market. Now is the time to perform the next set of actions and then start defining your purpose.

ACTION ITEMS

1. Check the skills list and the template to identify the skills you already have, the ones you need to master and the ones you have to improve.

2. Map the skills needed to achieve the goals in your Personal Development Plan.

3. Discuss with your leader how to combine the identified skills with the ones the company is expecting you to have. Make these skills complete each other and show it to your leader to create understanding and commitment.

2

Creating Purpose

Strategy is simply a bridge between vision and action/results/ winning.
—Thomas D. Zweifel

Leaders that lead with purpose "own" their standards for success, and are focused on objectives beyond task, job role or immediate business needs. Leaders with purpose define success as more than business and financial goals. They want to leave a legacy.

Those having a strong and clear sense of purpose do not need to share it with all members in the organization, but leaders need to translate their goals and objectives into something meaningful for their teams, co-workers, customers, and stakeholders.

We have all experienced situations in life where we felt lost and did not know where to go or how to accomplish what we wanted. Organizations and individuals willing to succeed understand the meaning of their actions and projects; it is the key to attaining performance and creating meaningful jobs. We are all searching for meaning, and more than ever the value of authentic leadership purpose is being mentioned in articles and leadership programs.

Identifying one's purpose and mission in life is energizing and motivating. Your career is your journey and you need to pack your own bag for this journey. I have learned that one essential part of my inventory that has to be in the bag is my purpose.

Defining your leadership purpose will help you improve your effectiveness and create great results. An authentic leadership purpose is connected to personal purpose and values. They are not merely statements; authentic leadership purposes have to lead to smart goals and create positive results. They create growth. They are an invitation to action!

Understanding the definitions

Let's explore some definitions and examples at an organizational level and then apply what we learn to form our own statements, purpose and vision.

Vision Statement: This is what your company aspires to be; which can be much different than what a company is (mission statement). Your vision statement can and should help drive decisions and goals in your company. A vision should be a source of inspiration.

Coca Cola presents it like that on its website:

"Our Vision

Our vision serves as the framework for our Roadmap and guides every aspect of our business by describing what we need to accomplish to continue achieving sustainable, quality growth.

- **People:** Be a great place to work where people are inspired to be the best they can be.

- **Portfolio:** Bring to the world a portfolio of quality beverage brands that anticipate and satisfy people's desires and needs.

- **Partners:** Nurture a winning network of customers and suppliers, together we create mutual, enduring value.

- **Planet:** Be a responsible citizen that makes a difference by helping build and support sustainable communities.

- **Profit:** Maximize long-term return to shareowners while being mindful of our overall responsibilities.

- **Productivity:** Be a highly effective, lean and fast-moving organization."

Mission Statement: This is what your company does. It should be short and easy to memorize. Coca Cola explains it very well:

"Our Mission
Our Roadmap starts with our mission, which is enduring. It declares our purpose as a company and serves as the standard against which we weigh our actions and decisions.

- To refresh the world...

- To inspire moments of optimism and happiness...

- To create value and make a difference."

Core Values: They are what support the vision, shape the culture, and reflect your company standards. They are your company's principles, beliefs, or philosophy of values. Companies normally limit their core values to five. Here are the values of Avon:

"**Belief** is the cornerstone of empowering Associates to assume responsibilities and be the very best they can be. Believe in someone – and show it – and that person will move mountains to prove you're right.

Integrity should be the hallmark of every Avon Associate. In setting and observing the highest ethical standards and doing the right thing, we fulfill a duty of care, not only to our Representatives and customers in the communities we serve, but to our colleagues and ourselves.

Respect helps us to value differences, to appreciate each person for her or his unique qualities. Through respect, we help bring out the full potential of each person.

Trust means we want to live and work in an environment where communications are open – where people feel free to take risks, to share their points of view and to speak the truth as they see it. Trust people to do the right thing – and help them to understand your underlying reasoning and philosophy – and they won't disappoint.

Humility simply means we're not always right – we don't have all the answers – and we know it. We're no less human than the people who work for us, and we're not afraid to ask for help."

Now that you have refreshed your knowledge about organizational vision, mission and values, let's think about your career vision, mission and values. They should reflect your personal purpose, source of inspiration, compass for your actions and guidelines for how you behave in life.

Creating a mission statement

We each have different roles in our lives, and we have responsibilities in different areas. I may have a role as an executive assistant, board member, wife, daughter, sister, neighbor, colleague, church member and more. And each of these roles is important. I am a collection of roles and therefore my goals have to embrace all the functions I have in society. My professional success depends on my personal life. My personal success is part of my professional performance.

A mission statement becomes a framework for thinking, for governing your acts and behaviour. Just as many organizations put their vision and mission statement on a wall and website, we need to do the same with our personal mission statement. Just as a company plans its strategy and activities based on the organization's mission, we all as individuals have our action plans anchored on our mission statement. A mission statement is based on values and priorities. It is unique, individual, and aligns behavior with beliefs.

A mission statement describes an organization's purpose and is related to the questions "What business are we in?" and "What is our business for?" A vision statement provides a strategic path and defines what the owner or founder wants the company to achieve in the future. Organizations willing to succeed need to know where they are going or why they exist. We, as individuals, also need to know our "why", "what" and "how".

There is no strategy without a vision. So, remember that "first a dream, then a vision and a mission, and because of all that, we create a strategy to fulfill the dream."

What are you here for? What are your dreams? Before you start defining your career strategy, you must answer these questions. So, it is time again to take your pen and start doing a new exercise. If you need more space to your answers, expand the boxes below by using post-its. Write as many words as necessary to make the answers as complete as possible. This is a brainstorming process and I want you to enjoy each part of it.

Who are you? (Both privately and professionally.)

What legacy do you want to leave? (Both privately and professionally.)

What are you here for?

What are your dreams?

Sharing my vision and leadership purpose

Defining my leadership as an Executive Assistant was a process that included introspection and reflection. I went through my education, skills, life experiences, dreams, feedback and performance reviews. I listed my values and main personal and professional objectives. All of that was to ensure an authentic leadership purpose that would be practiced daily. In this process I asked myself some crucial questions:

What are my values?

- Honesty
- Loyalty
- Commitment
- Quality
- Structure
- Freedom
- Respect

What do I want to contribute to the organization?

I want to maximize the productivity of my executives and teams.

What is my desired impact?

- Create a partnership between Executive and Executive Assistant;
- Make a difference to my executives;

- Inspire and motivate my teams;
- Do the work they delegate to me and allow them to dedicate their time to core business;
- Read the mind of my executives.

How can my executives help me attain my desired impact?

I need them to:

- Delegate;
- Communicate;
- Trust;
- Share their goals and priorities;
- Give feedback;
- Explain the WHY.

What is my vision?

There is no strategy without a vision.

A vision is what inspires us to imagine the unimaginable, to go the extra mile. Your vision will help you plan accordingly, engage people around you, energize you, help you exceed and succeed.

- Where are you now?
- Where are you going?
- How will you get there?

With a vision you can go far. My vision statement is a source of inspiration and motivation. It's what I want to achieve. That's my present and my future. It's shaping my future and my career. It's giving me direction. It inspires me!

When you are making strategic decisions for your career development and even daily private and professional decisions, your vision statement will give you the inspiration and targeted direction you need. Without a vision statement, you will lack motivation to keep going, keeping building a successful future for your career. Your vision has to be shaped every day. It is like a muscle. It is more than a dream. It is the force that will make your dream come true.

#BeTheBestAssistant
PERFORMING AT A HIGHER LEVEL

What is my leadership purpose?

"I will continuously and consistently develop and facilitate the growth and development of myself and others leading to great performance and positive results."

You will find my leadership purpose on my LinkedIn profile. I also had it hanging on the whiteboard in my office. I want everyone, not only myself, to promote my leadership purpose and help me attain my goals. It needs to be a constant focal point leading me to the right career decisions and priorities. My leadership purpose is about who I am, not only about something I do. It is part of my career strategy. It is helping me be intentionally strategic in everything I do.

Embracing audaciousness

Garry Kasparov emphasizes the importance of combining intelligence with audaciousness in any strategic plan with these words: "Ultimately, what separates a winner from a loser at the grandmaster level is the willingness to do the unthinkable. A brilliant strategy is, certainly, a matter of intelligence, but intelligence without audaciousness is not enough."

So, any successful leadership purpose and mission have to be combined with a certain level of boldness, and being willing to undertake things that involve risk. A purpose that embraces audaciousness is a purpose that is ready to question the status quo, and thrive in an unpredictable and rapidly changing environment.

Bringing audaciousness to your career strategy means:

- Challenging the traditional nations;

- Finding new winning combinations;

- Embracing and thriving in new or complex positions;

- Having the unique ability to adapt;

- Finding new opportunities;

- Thinking outside the box.

These six elements are required when thinking about the future of work and building an ultimate career strategy. As the world of work is changing, the way we think «our work» has to change too. Organizations and employees should not just want to survive, they must want to thrive and be competitive in a new rapidly changing world.

Challenge the traditional notions

Any strategic career plan has to be based on eliminating the traditional ways of doing things to create innovative ways of working and adding value. In this age of our fourth industrial revolution, rapid technological and social change in an increasing number of economic sectors are approaching a tipping point at which companies must become agile to survive. The time when we could build strategy planning that would stay relevant for five to ten years is over. Any disruptive idea generating disruptive business is creating a market which initially didn't exist, or providing a better product to the ignored less-demanding consumers. So, challenging the traditional notions is all about understanding the need for boosting your career with disruptive ideas, skills and performance that will transform you into a competitive employee.

Imagine that your existing market, your company and industry, has any sort of scarcity. Start identifying and studying which skills or behavior you need to be able to offer something more powerful to the market.

Look for what can be improved in your existing market, and think about how you can provide a more sustainable product or service to your customers (your managers). Can you come up with an idea that serves both the un-served as well as the mass market in a better way than they are presently being served? If your answer is YES, then you have all the reasons you need to go ahead in creating a career strategy that will allow you to deliver the service your market and customers really need.

Find new winning combinations

One of my personal examples regarding creating winning combinations through career strategy is when I volunteered as Chairman of the Board at IMA Norway – International Management Assistants. One of the things that motivated me to go the extra mile was the positive impact of seeing my ideas and initiatives – and the achievements of my members – being spread throughout the association.

Connecting the dots for me during these two years was like finding a common thread that encompassed the issues, ideas and resources in my national group and my workplace. My executives supported my voluntary work, enabling me to be an ambassador for my company when also representing the association at national and international events. My past work experience as a teacher, salesperson and marketer helped me to drive positive results and see things with different perspectives. I could improve our new members' onboarding process, implement a strategic planning routine, improve the business relations with corporate members and make our members aware of their role as stakeholders. This experience is opening the doors I need to evolve professionally and keep having a sustainable career.

Embrace and thrive in new or complex positions

During my professional career, I have had the privilege of working with great leaders and mentors. They were – and are – continually offering me opportunities to learn leadership from seeing them in action and being their business partner. It has been a real leadership school. Leading IMA (International Management Assistants) Norway, I was again being given a chance to keep developing and practicing my leadership skills – and extending my learning arena outside the corporate context. I could combine my demanding role as Executive Assistant with the position as IMA Norway's National Chairman, writer, public speaker, mentor and Wellbeing Ambassador because everything I did was helping me grow and become a better version of myself.

Have the unique ability to adapt

To ensure your growth in the face of change we need to be continually challenging and adapting old ways of thinking while pushing ourselves just beyond our comfort zone. The ability to adapt is a must-have quality for any employee or professional willing to have a successful career. We all know that things change and that the only thing constant is change. Every day we experience the impact of the evolution of employment and skills in the age of AI (artificial intelligence). The transformation of how we work embraces all industries and all jobs. Administrative professionals are not alone in enduring the impact of technology. We all need to stay alert and vigilant in a positive way.

It's up to you to be adaptable! And what gives us the ability to adapt is our capability to anticipate future trends in our industry, be curious, always be learning, keep on sharping our critical thinking, and knowing our vision.

To successfully learn how to deal with change and embrace adaptability, you need to know where you're going.

Find new opportunities

Slip into a new role – don't wait for permission! By slipping into a new role you can change your perspective and the way you think about things drastically. A new department can mean new opportunities, new colleagues, new perspectives and certainly a step towards your dream role.

When you with consistency embrace challenge, learning and failing, you are preparing yourself for new opportunities. Embracing new roles and working with new people will help you extend your circle of colleagues. You will be extending your network, developing relationships with influencers and thought-leaders within and outside your organization, sharing, supporting, listening, learning and contributing to people's growth.

Most people don't think about their work as a career or even a choice. Most people see their work as tedious or as a necessary means to be able to provide for themselves and others. For me, my work has to be associated with joy and passion, challenge and growth, and a journey of audaciousness. What if you:

- Look at your work as a choice that you make intentionally?

- See your professional career as a journey that will make you run into some obstacles, failures, victories, challenges, ups and downs, before you land in the field that fits you?

At the end of 2015, I accepted one of the most exciting challenges in my career journey. I said yes to the invitation to speak to executive assistants at a conference in Stockholm, Sweden that took place in February 2016. The title of the talk was "My Personal View: Assistant Now And In The Future." This activity was related to my long-term goal to become a public speaker and a more confident presenter in executive meetings.

Before accepting, I asked my CEO for the authorization to be absent for two days and to have my presentation linked to my role at the company. Then I contacted the organiser and confirmed the speaking engagement. Some weeks later, I started researching to define the content of the talk. I read books and articles, especially about public speaking (a skill I wanted to improve). I worked on refining my speaking abilities and participated in a training session with a communications expert together with members of the executive team – a win-win situation. I also had an extra coaching session to finalise the presentation tactics.

My speaking coach helped me develop the idea of starting my presentation by making people dance samba and sing and dance a folkloric Swedish song – which made my talk unforgettable for many. I prepared the slides and started memorizing the content. One week before the seminar, I sent my slides to the organiser and felt prepared for the next step of the challenge: present to an audience with over hundred participants. The talk was a success, and I received a high rate of positive feedback.

Public speaking can be a great self-esteem booster, gives opportunities to meet new social and professional contacts, is an effective platform for spreading revolutionary ideas, and enhances critical thinking.

A peer and member of the association IMA – International Management Assistants, said to me once that the job of Management Assistant prepares you for any assignment. Her words confirm what I always have though about the jobs I have had. Each one of them were preparing me for something bigger.

So, think about your career as a mosaic of opportunities that are building your professional future. Be strategic, intentional and proactive.

Think outside the box

When planning your strategy, think outside the box, think global. Progress is not linear but comes in evolutionary leaps. You will need freedom to experiment and play, and the freedom to fail. Build your career strategy based on your career philosophy, creating it every day. "You cannot see very far into the future, but you have a vison, and push for that vision with decisive action every day" wrote Thomas D. Zweifel, author and leadership expert.

Audaciousness is about being brave, adventurous and challenging yourself. I was once very audacious when I was headhunted to become a sales and marketing coordinator for an online Norwegian course and accepted the challenge. They saw my values and potential, maybe not me. So, I asked the interviewer:

"Why are you asking me, an Executive Assistant who has never been a salesperson and know nothing about sales and marketing, to take on this so important role?"

They listed all my skills and one of them was my international background, my language knowledge and the fact of being myself a foreigner who had to learn the Norwegian language. I was the best trademark for the product.

This role was one of the most exciting ones I have had in terms of learning complete new skills and building my career to the top. I learned and practiced communication skills, strategic prospecting, budgeting, negotiation skills, advertising, and public speaking.

I could not have had the successful career I have today without this experience in sales and marketing. Thinking outside the box is more than just a business cliché. It means approaching problems in new, innovative ways, conceptualizing problems differently, and understanding your position in relation to any particular situation in a way you'd never thought of before. And the four and a half years working as sales and marketing advisor gave me a uniqueness that few assistants have.

ACTION ITEMS

1. To help you define your core values I recommend you visit the website stevepavlina.com and check the list of values.
2. List your values based on the list or what you already know about what is important for you.
3. Ask people who know you well to help you define your list of core values.
4. Create your mission.
5. Define your vision and check this site for inspiration:
List of Values https://www.stevepavlina.com/blog/2004/11/list-of-values/

3

Aligning the Goals

Coming together is a beginning. Keeping together is progress.
Working together is success.
– Henry Ford

We spend most part of our day at work. We dedicated most time of our day to support our executives and teams. Therefore, the best way for us to get our career strategy up and running is by having our goals aligned with our manager's goals. The better we work together, the better we will benefit of the hours we spend together. Building a successful relationship with our executives is key for our career success and the execution of the strategy.

Alignment gives us balance, harmony and enables collaboration. The word alignment is also defined as:

"an agreement between a group of countries, political parties, or people who want to work together because of shared interests or aims."

– Cambridge Dictionary.

Understanding your executive's goals

As business partners, the Executive and Assistant have to be extremely conscious of the impact they have when their activities are linked. Knowing the executive's goals is crucial to all assistants. It allows optimized performance and maximum output. Understanding the objectives your executive has to accomplish will help ensure consistency among tasks and initiatives.

- Do you know your executive's goals for the year?

- Have you asked your executive how you can help him or her to deliver?

- Do you brief each other about the main ongoing projects?

- Do you have a one page ready at all times containing the talking points on your major projects? (Your projects have to be the projects that will ensure the results your executive has to deliver.)

- Are you able to cover your manager's blind spot?

For some years, one of my strategic career goals was improving my communication skills and becoming a public speaker. This goal was aligned with one of the organizational goals: improve internal communication. To support my CEO in getting the desired results in this area, I added to my PDP (Personal Development Plan) two important strategic activities: have a minimum of two public speaking engagements associated to my role as National Chairman of IMA Norway, and write articles to our company intranet. To succeed in these activities, I defined some day-to-day operational tasks as:

- interviewing colleagues from different departments to know more about our business, products and services;

- reading books about leadership and writing more articles for administrative professionals on the topic;

- attending sessions with a communication coach.

All of these activities were supported by my employer because they were clearly aligned with my executive's and organization's goals. A perfect win-win situation all round. Also, the feeling of developing myself according to my own career aspirations kept me engaged and productive.

I felt passionate about my job, was committed to the organization, and put discretionary effort into my work every single day. I left this company because I received the opportunity to keep growing professionally in the role of Chief Human Resources Officer – a dream job.

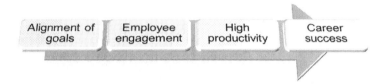

Know your organization's strategy

A business is best aligned when the interests of all stakeholders in the business are in alliance with the strategic objectives.

- Are you able to summarize the company's business?

- Have you read your company's strategy?

- Are you taking part in strategy meetings?

- Is your job description reflecting the overall strategy and your executive's objectives?

Mastering the above will help you become a true business partner and consequently enhance your relationship with your executive.

Extending your business partnership to the next level

Being able to align your career strategy with your company's strategy will show that you are able to extend your business partnership with your managers and executives to the highest level of a successful alliance.

As mentioned in the previous chapters, all successful career strategy has to be linked to continuous learning, creative thinking, and audaciousness. These elements will help us feel comfortable in "stepping into new worlds." It is one of the most efficient ways to change our perspective and to discover insights that remained completely unknown to us. Stepping into new worlds will help us extend our business partnership with our executives and managers to the next level. Building a successful career takes time, effort, and patience. It involves everything we do, our choices, attitudes and behaviours both in our private and professional life.

Here are some activities that will boost your business partnership:

- Find a new hobby;

- Meet new people;

- Gather knowledge about topics that interest you;

- Study another industry;

- Study a new language;

- Take classes.

I embraced a new hobby for four years ago: writing. Today I am writing articles for the Executive Secretary Magazine and blogs. I was also writing my CEO's articles for the company's intranet. This is because I went out of my comfort zone, developed a natural skill I have and applied it to everything I do, privately and professionally.

I also decided to study business administration as part of my career strategy. I wanted to deliver at a higher and more strategic level. I did it! I was congratulated by my executive when I decided to take the last certification, Finance Management, and got if funded by the company.

So now I want you to do some homework before we continue reading this book. I want you to identify five actions that you are going to implement to your day-to-day operations to extend your business partnership with your executive or manager:

Action	Purpose

Selling your career strategic plan

Use all the information you have now gathered about yourself and your company's strategic plan to build a solid case complete with specific examples, trends, and likely outcomes.

Go to this conversation armed with current data and projections for future results. You have to show the importance of aligning your career goals with the organizations' goals, and how you can complement each other. It is all about creating synergy and enabling growth. The success of this conversation will depend on how effective you are in explaining to your managers how you can keep on adding value.

It is all about communication

Use your one-to-one meetings to ask questions and learn more about your company's strategy and its related activities. Everyone understands a well-communicated strategy at some level. Be the person who helps the top management communicate and filter the strategy.

Once as a team leader for a group of management assistants, I invited my VP to present and explain the organization's strategy to all of the assistants. The VP helped everyone to understand the strategy in terms of their own day to day work.

Sometimes the main challenge is presented by a plan that is too difficult to be easily understood by all employees. Ask yourself:

- Is everyone "getting it"?

- How can I help the executive team to communicate our strategy plan?

- How often am I sitting together with my leaders to ask about the priorities and challenges?

- Am I curious enough to ask good questions?

Strategy planning is not a solo game. Collaboration is a key word and good communication will improve collaboration. When we know the "Why" and "What", it becomes easy to align objectives and define the "How."

Here are some examples:

- Seize opportunities to work on cross-functional, even virtual, teams, that solve a problem or approach new opportunities. Embrace the very ethos of "constant change". Be inspired to be more open to adopting the latest tech innovations in the future. Take the initiative to seek training and education to develop your individual capacity, and increase your skill-set.

- Create an open conversation arena with your executive and ask for ideas about how you can become better at what you are delivering. Create a relationship that is based on business partnership, shared values and common goals.

- Train your executive to think about you as his or her best business partner. A partnership based on shared values, cooperation, growth, effective communication and openness is crucial in helping you prioritize your tasks and goals when new strategic initiatives are added to the agenda. It will allow you to fix issues faster, show work as it develops and learn together.

- Ask your executive to keep you informed about strategic plans and problems to be addressed. You can be one of the contributors in finding innovative solutions to these problems. Make your executive understand that he is also responsible for creating an environment that allows you to maintain focus on the critical priorities and assist the team in an agile way.

- Make a list of the skills you have that complement your executive's skills. Map the new skills you need to acquire to improve the level of partnership you currently have.

- Create partnerships with teams, colleagues, mentors, and like-minded assistants. They will allow you to proactively identify and pursue opportunities to develop in your daily work. Meet these people on a regular basis for stand-up meetings or brainstorming. Pair up to design, test, manage or simply explore new ideas together. Create a learning program and meet regularly in a formal and informal manner.

- Create a culture of feedback (either formally or informally) on your behavior, progress and outcomes. This is what we call performance orientation. It is crucial to create agility in changing or adapting where necessary, before you expend precious time in a task, product or service that is not going to create a satisfactory outcome. Continuous feedback is crucial for alignment and career development.

- Be accountable for your results and know that there are consequences for met and unmet goals. I recommend that you share your accomplishments with your executive during your one-on-one meetings. Include this "accomplishments review" as a fixed part of your conversations. It will create a strong sense of collaboration. Your managers are likely to support your goal accomplishment as your success is their success. In addition, add an "actions review" routine. Go through the tasks and actions you have in your performance development plan (PDP) as often as possible. It will allow you to "adjust" the actions, to modify or eliminate them when necessary in order to keep delivering according to the priorities.

The more you share what you have accomplished, learned, created and developed to add value to the business, the more you will strengthen your business partnership with your executives and managers, and the more you will be contributing mutually to your career development.

Taking ownership

Career progression is a crucial factor to ensure employees remain productive and engaged within the workplace. A salary research made by Hays reveals that "along with salary and benefit packages, 27 percent of professional say the main reason for wanting to leave their role is due to a lack of future opportunities."

- Are you willing to go above and beyond the job specification and proactively solve problems and identify new solutions?

- Do you have specific industry experience and knowledge?

- Do you have any specific function experience and knowledge such as HR, Finance, Communications, Marketing or Social Media?

When you take ownership, and practice your leadership skills every day, you will be able to become a strategic enabler. A dynamic career has to reflect the pace of change we are experiencing. The pace of change is accelerating, and this will not stop. "Talent" no longer means the same as it did ten years ago; many of the roles, skills and job titles of tomorrow are unknown to us today.

So, start taking ownership now! Own the automation debate and learn about what it means for the business and the industry you belong to! Automation and Artificial Intelligence (AI) will affect every level of your business and its people. This means that it will affect you, the way you work, the tools you use, the tasks assigned, the way you communicate with your colleagues, the way you adapt to change, nurture agility, adaptability and re-skilling.

There is a value in what you do for your organization

When I started in my position as Executive Assistant to the CEO and founder of an IT company, one of the first tasks I added to my to-do list was read the company's strategy. I read it with interest, took notes, formulated questions, checked the meaning of technical terminologies and definitions, and drafted an action plan template that would help the CEO follow up the strategic actions across departments. I was applying knowledge from a previous position, when I actively participated in organizational strategic planning as a member of the management team. By doing that, I showed my executive at what level I was able to contribute to the success of the organization. She understood that I was "much more than an Executive Assistant."

Become a strategic enabler

The *Executive-and-Assistant Strategic Alignment* focuses energy, eliminates redundancy, removes conflicting work and defines the capabilities and competencies, which provide strategic synergy.

How can the Assistant help her or his Executive achieve specific goals related to the organization's strategy?

- Take accountability and be engaged. The organizations strategy is also YOUR strategy.

- List all actions that you can perform to help the executive accomplish their goals.

- Keep networking. It will help you to know how the strategy is being understood and communicated by the rest of the organization.

- Understand your job description and make it reflect the organization's goals.

- Remove obstacles. Take ownership for as many tasks as possible from the executive's to-do list. It will give your executive more time to focus on the strategy plan. There are many activities assistants can do on behalf of their executives, for example handling e-mails, sharing information, leading and attending meetings, defining meeting agendas, making decisions and initiating projects.

- Make your executive know that your efforts matter!

Before the beginning of the tenure of my new CEO, at the end of 2016, I decided to prepare the onboarding plan to accelerate his own leadership and team's success in the first critical days and beyond. The plan would also help him access the business context and internal political culture he would be facing in his new role. As I started in the company in 2015, I still had my own onboarding accelerator plan fresh in my memory and notes. It gave me motivation and the relevant background to be able to prepare the onboarding plan of my new CEO.

Firstly, I decided to gather information by reading the book 'The First 90 Days – Proven Strategies for Getting Up to Speed Faster and Smarter' to help me select the actions I would add in the onboarding plan for my new CEO. I wanted to anticipate the activities and plan them accordingly. After checking the company's onboarding checklist to identify the responsible persons for the actions, I determined the actions I could do and added new activities to the guideline. I also read many articles about the onboarding of CEOs.

While editing the onboarding manual, which included much more than an office set-up checklist, I talked with my HR colleagues to ensure that the plan was aligned with the organization's onboarding strategy. I also presented the idea to the Chair of the Board, one of the main stakeholders in the process, and got her appreciation for being proactive. Doing everything right and in a timely manner would help us to ensure effective communication planning, leadership team pre-start alignment, clarification of expectations, and jump-start key relationships and accelerate learning, among other benefits.

When I finalised the guideline, I presented it to the new CEO. He was very satisfied and started collaborating with me, while still in his former position, in adding some activities as suggestions for one-on-one meetings, access to company information and equipment before the start day, and preparation of the all-hands meeting.

Some of the outcomes of this initiative were that:

- The guideline helped me have control along the process and give us clarity and understanding of what we were doing – enhancing our partnership Executive & Executive Assistant and ensuring alignment.

- It also helped me facilitate the onboarding of another executive, our CTO.

- This exercise inspired me to revise my own onboarding strategy manual – a win-win situation.

- It inspired me to share my tips for accelerating the onboarding process and write an article for executive assistants with the title "New job? Now what?! (http://executivesecretary.com/new-job-now-what/)

Commitment to Learning

One of the different ways to have your goals aligned with your executive's goals is by creating a learning strategy that will allow you to get the necessary skills to enable an *Executive and Executive Assistant synergy.*

How can you practice your commitment to learning?

Boost curiosity. It will keep your interest in deep reflection and continuous inquiry and learning. Learning happens at all stages of life development and not only in educational or professional settings. Learning also happen in homes, study groups, online courses, conferences, workshops, libraries, community centers, and other settings.

Curiosity, reflection, tolerance of failure and vulnerability, feedback, and systems thinking are important to the culture of learning.

Curiosity self-assessment

- Reflect about the ideas that energize and make you wonder.

- What are you curious about?

- What do you want or need to know more about?

- What would your executive or manager like you to know more about?

- What do you need to be curious about to grow professionally?

Making learning a lifelong habit is key for all professional development strategy. All employees must be committed to learning. It must become a habit and be part of your career development. In addition to that, we must implement learning immediately and perform tasks we have learned as soon as possible.

When attending conferences, workshops or online training, you should be very attentive to writing down specific takeaways and actions to be performed immediately after the event. Research shows that performing the tasks you have learned is crucial because performing enhances memory and serves as an elaborative encoding strategy. So whatever field you choose to study to enhance your expertise or learn new skills, find opportunities to use your new skill.

- Ask to be part of a project team;

- Volunteer;

- Set up your own project;

- Create an action plan.

Focus on emerging skills when making a self-assessment, to identify the short and long-term improvement areas. You are refining yourself for your current position and for the future. Ask yourself how successful you want to be. List your improvement goals and make a plan to attain the objectives through learning and development. Align your training plan with the goals of your department and executive.

When planning which conferences and online training you are going to attend, think about bringing to the workplace something new that you can put immediately into practice after the training session, and highlight the topics in the event program that motivate you, a speaker whose book you have read, professionals from your industry that you want to connect with, strategic persons that can mentor you or the presentation of smart tools that will boost your efficiency. See the whole picture and study all the possibilities. List all the advantages you will get from the selected training events. Align them with the goals you have identified.

Being aligned with your executive or management will allow you to boost your career at any time. It will allow you to "be responsible for your own professional development, ensure you have the skills you need now, and take opportunities to expand and grow those skills whenever you can, so that you are ready for the next opportunity that presents itself to you", as Eth Lloyd, Chair of the World Administrators Summit 2018, brilliantly said in the interview for my site Organizational Health and Wellbeing for Assistants.

Professor Barbara Oakley said that "people can often do more, change more, and learn more – often far more – than they've ever dreamed possible and that "our potential is hidden in plain sight all around us." So, alignment is all about harmonizing your skills-set in accordance with shared interests and organizational aims.

The most successful companies get all their moving parts working in alignment with each other to achieve their top objectives in a manner consistent with their core values and priorities. The most successful Executive Assistants make an all-out effort to be in sync with the organization's goals by supporting and empowering their executives.

Interdependent people combine their own efforts with the efforts of others to achieve their greatest success, said Stephen Covey, author of the best-seller 'The 7 Habits of Highly Effective People'.

ACTION ITEMS

1. Identify your company's three top strategic goals and main strategic areas.
2. Translate your team and department goals and priorities into concrete action steps that can be performed by you.
3. Schedule a one-on-one meeting with your executive or manager to present your concrete action steps and make them know that you understand the company's goals and priorities. Tell them how you want to contribute to the success of the company's strategy.

4

Executing the Actions

Plans are only good intentions unless they immediately degenerate into hard work."
– Peter Drucker

Strategic planning and goal setting must be linked with everyone on the team having goals that support the plan and each other. It is not a solo game. It is all about joint forces. The same applies to the execution of your career strategy. Some people say that "Execution is the Strategy" because in today's world of rapid and disruptive constant change, strategy has to be connected to execution and emerge from execution. A successful tool for execution is the ability to leverage your talents, others' talents, involve the best people, boost collaboration, create alignments, embrace agility, and prioritize the right strategic actions and operational activities.

Yes! Your career strategy is full of operational activities, the actions you have to perform daily in order to achieve your career goals. It is all about turning strategy into performance.

Shared understanding

Key stakeholders from all segments of the company come together to face facts and forge a shared understanding of the future situation. Viewing the big picture together as a team – even if the team is your executive and you – will boost execution process. It means being on the same page. It is a result of alignment. You already know what is possible to achieve; you have a vision and mission purpose that is aligned with your organization's goals. The alignment is a kind of magnet that pulls the present to the future, big enough to energize you.

As an Executive Assistant and part of the management team, I know I am one of the organization's leaders. We must remember that leaders can be at all levels of the organization. The author and leadership expert Thomas D.

Zweifel defines four types of leaders involved in strategic process:

- Those who lead the strategic process itself, typically Board members and C-level executives;

- Implementers;

- Other affected stakeholders;

- Gatekeepers who might throw a wrench into the process unless they are aligned.

So now ask yourself which kind of leader you are in the strategic process.

- For your career strategy, are you leading the process itself?

- In your organization, are you part of the C-suit team? If yes, are you really leading the process alongside your executives?

- If you are an implementer, are you taking the responsibility for making things happen?

- Do you feel you are only a gatekeeper?

If you want to be the CEO of your career strategy, and are not there yet, now is the time to take the lead. Use this book as a source of motivation and starting point for defining your strategy.

Now say it loud: It is time to take the lead! Taking the lead means also being hands-on and being an active player in the execution of the strategy.

Strategy can be broken down into mini-tasks and preformed predictably. This is one of the most heard sentences regarding strategy planning. At an organizational level, one example of that is when the different functions are asked to present their contribution to the strategy. This is typical top-down strategic planning. As a career strategic planner I can share with you my break-down tactic for growing myself as a writer.

Here is a summary of my strategy plan for becoming a writer.

The intentions	Strategic actions
• Improve communication skills; • Improve fluency in English; • Share knowledge; • Empower and inspire others; • Grow professionally and personally.	• Choose two main focus areas per year (example: The Agile Mindset , Organizational Health and Wellbeing, Career Development); • Write six articles per year for blogs and magazines related to the main focus areas; • Share quotes from the books I am reading on LinkedIn; • Proactively search for relevant topics and write articles to the company's intranet; • Publish articles on my profile on LinkedIn.

The results of this strategy are that today I am writing this book, sharing my top tips with you on how to build a strong career strategy, and contributing and adding value to our community of administrative professionals.

I also became a respected employee among my colleagues due to the relevant content of articles and posts I am publishing on LinkedIn. The vision motivating me to perform my strategy actions with passion and purpose was #BeTheBestAssistant.

We need people

"You can start being strategic daily through one simple practice: be a connector," said Steve Browne, an accomplished speaker, writer, and thought leader on Human Resource Management. People are the most important things in executing strategies. They can bring enthusiasm and energy to the process. People can collaborate and make great results happen. But they can also sabotage your action plan. Everyone has a value and we have to tap into these values, make people join forces and build great things together. Your career strategy has to be able to gather the best people you may need to build a brilliant professional future for you.

- Surround yourself with positive people.

- Have a community that gives you different perspectives.

- Have an accountability partner.

- Create your board of directors.

- Share what you learn.

- Support people in attaining their goals.

- Be a bridge.

- Intentionally spend time with people who are different from you.

To make the right people stay with you and support your career plans, you have to build your relationships from people's strengths. This accelerates growth, boosts enthusiasm, enhances trust and collaboration, and creates engagement.

- Be a connector! Connect people to your dreams, vision, purpose and work.

- Look at each interaction with people in your workplace as a chance to bring a solution and to plant some seeds of encouragement to get through struggle.

- What can you learn from the people you meet?

We need each other to grow personally and professionally. We all want to experience a sense of community. I know that because I was a member of a fantastic association for support management professionals. I could not have succeeded professionally without my peers.

My family has also played a significant role in my career development. They were my first network, advisors, supporters and partners. They were seeing my talents and helping me design career strategy actions, making me think outside the box, go beyond my limits. This was the foundation for everything!

My first job was as a teacher in Brazil. I worked as a teacher in both private and public schools. Very early, my mother realized my talent for languages. I started learning English and French at a high level when I was twelve years old. Later, I started studying Spanish. I have a Bachelor's degree in Portuguese and French Language and Literature. I also have a Master's degree in French Language and Literature from the University of Nancy and a Master's degree in Portuguese Language and Literature from the University of Oslo. I come from a family where we were all encouraged to improve our talents and be the best we can be. I am who I am today because of my dedicated and supportive family. I could not be who I am today without everything my parents did to give us the best education and opportunities.

The art of networking is no longer something to be ignored. We will be stronger as a profession the more we are connected. The current workforce is global, connected, mobile, transient, and multi-generational. With social media, your network can literally be global. As the two authors, Stephen R. Covey and Jennifer Colosimo wrote, "it's a natural principle that you cannot achieve anything truly worthwhile alone – at least not in the world of work."

Operational, Personal, and Strategic Networks

You need operational, personal and strategic networks to get things done, to develop personally and professionally. The operation network will help you to complete your professional tasks and perform effectively. Your personal network will help you to detox, have fun and link you to your family, friends and the friends of your friends. It is linked to your personal goals and affinities. Your strategic network will help you to follow a career path, find new projects at work, connect your executive with potential customers, discover the new trends in the industry, generate breakthrough ideas and avoid group thinking, among many other opportunities. It helps you to envision the future. If you have a plan for your career, you must embrace strategic-network-thinking.

Examples of operational networks for assistants are the different professional groups and associations. Networks provide us with the opportunity to share ideas, concerns, information and resources, aspirations and ideals.

How my network helped me improve public speaking skills

Here are some strategic actions for you if you intend to become a good speaker:

- Start by becoming a member of a network where people have the opportunity to speak out.

- Hold short presentations and interact with different kind of professionals.

- Transform this network opportunity into a practicing arena.

- Find a subject of interest, tell others that you have good practices to share that can help others to succeed and determine the time to hold your presentation.

- The next step? Find a new subject of interest, tell others that you want to share your best practices and tips, and the rest you know.

This is only one example of how you can think network in a strategic way. Be strategically intentional!

How Diverse is Your Strategic Network?

We know that research supports the notion that people who are connected across heterogeneous groups and who have more-diverse contacts come up with more creative ideas and original solutions. So, let's do a self-assessment exercise to help us define strategic actions to improve the diversity of our networks.

- Who are the people you are spending time with? (Ages, cultures, religions, education, industries, geographic locations and other distinctions.)

- List up to ten persons with whom you have discussed important work matters over the past few months.

- What are the main strengths and weaknesses of your professional network?

- Who are the new people you need to meet?

- Have you ever thought about joining networks related to other profession than the one you currently represent?

- What are the ways you're interacting day in and day out with your colleagues, clients, other professionals and industry partners?

Now, I want you to create a strategic action plan that will help you have a more diverse network. Think about actions that are easy to be implemented, that will keep you motivated and interested in building the right relationships.

Action	Purpose	Who can help you?	What do you need to get the action done quicker?

What about creating your own networking events?

If you wish to build a powerful strategic network, branch out. Build a diverse network of professional contacts that include people that don't look like you, sound like you, speak like you, or have your background, education, or history. The only thing that they should have in common with you and the other people in your network is that they should be really good at what they do.

A ROBUST STRATEGIC NETWORK WILL HELP YOU:

Having a tribe

Just imagine that you start in a new role, land your first job as an HR professional. A career path from Senior Executive Assistant to Chief Human Resources Officer. You need very quickly to build your onboarding strategy and how you will step up and take charge with confidence on day one. How could we facilitate this transition? I did it by searching for a Human Resources local Facebook group. I sent a request to join the group. I received a positive answer two days after my request was sent. Then I sent a message to the members saying:

"Hi everyone, I'm new to the group. Thank you for allowing me to join the group. I've got a new role as HR director in a Norwegian startup. I will build up the HR function in the company.

I am looking forward to the job and would like to meet more of you who have experience in the field."

Two weeks later, I had the pleasure of meeting one of the members, a young and enthusiastic HR director, who kindly volunteered to support me and become my mentor. In our first meeting, she shared her best tips on how I could start implementing the most important routines when building an HR department from scratch. I can tell you that this session was much better than just reading articles on the topic after some Google search results.

The point about this story is that people long to be connected. I need to be connected to grow professionally in a new field and my HR peer wants to be connected to empower others. We are better together!

Executing in an agile way

We live in an age of accelerating disruption. Every company is facing up the profound changes wrought by digitization. Globalization made commercialization practically borderless. Today, digitization is making industry boundaries permeable and almost invisible. Data, algorithms and artificial intelligence are changing the nature of strategy planning and execution, forecasting, decision making, and the workplace itself.

Each of us in our career strategy execution, no differently from companies, have to respond to disruptive times by rethinking our "business models", redesigning our careers, adopting an agile mindset, and embracing design thinking.

What is design thinking?

Design thinking is a method for practical, creative resolution of problems. It is a form of solution-focused thinking with the intent of producing a constructive future result.

Design thinking identifies and investigates both known and ambiguous aspects of the current situation in an effort to discover parameters and alternative solution sets which may lead to one or more satisfactory goals. Because design thinking is iterative, intermediate "solutions" are potential starting points of alternative paths, allowing for redefinition of the initial problem, in a process of co-evolution of problem and solution. (Wikipedia)

What is an agile mindset?

Being agile is about taking necessary risks, being innovative and rapidly finding new solutions, being flexible and embracing resilience. An agile mindset embraces collaboration at all levels. Agility has become one of the most popular, highly valued workplace concepts today, and hiring managers are in constant search for "agile" employees that will create "agile" organizations.

Being agile means having the ability to quickly adapt or evolve in response to changing circumstances. Being able to break down barriers in the workplace in order to meet changing business needs, advancements, or technologies is essential for any agile team. So your career strategy has to reflect an agile mindset.

A dynamic career needs a flexible and agile strategy! The pace of change is accelerating, and this will not stop. How can you execute your strategy in an agile way?

- Create a sharing and learning culture in your department and within your team.

- Embrace team collaboration inside and outside your organization.

- Start a network for assistants to brainstorm, exchange knowledge and innovative thinking.

- Go for social learning activities through peer-to-peer and online learning.

- Feel comfortable with uncertainty.

- Keep growing and expanding your knowledge base.

- Be part of an environment where it is safe to fail. Learn from your failures.

- Find new ways to do things. Be creative and innovative.

- Look beyond the present or a problem to see events from a broad and global perspective.

- Step forward and take risks.

- Try new tasks and roles.

- Break down barriers.

- Be resilient and enhance your capacity to bounce back in the face of stress, adversity or change.

- Create emphatic environments.

- Boost your ability to think clearly and rationally, being able to understand the logical connection between ideas.

- Be flexible and learn how to maintain productivity during transitions or periods of chaos.

Let's move quickly, move easily, and effectively!

I want to share with you my experience in fostering a learning culture in the workplace. Some years ago, I initiated a sharing and learning arena, the participants being my former colleagues working in the Finance, Administration and HR departments in our office in Oslo.

I decided to extend the sharing and learning sessions I was having with managers to accelerate my onboarding process. I wanted my colleagues to participate and have the chance to increase business understanding: what we are delivering to customers, who our customers are, what our ongoing projects are. Also, I wanted to have the opportunity to elicit questions and eliminate doubts.

I shared my idea with my colleagues and got their agreement. They were highly interested in learning more. After that, I chose a colleague to help me make a survey to map the preferred topics and contact the managers who would be available to hold the presentations. I made an agenda for the year giving priority to the most voted topics. I sent out invitations and launched the initiative officially. To keep the organization informed about the activities, I wrote some articles for our intranet, also showing gratitude for the time many managers dedicated to us in sharing their expertise. As a tech-savvy person, I also included a session to share with my colleagues some best Microsoft Outlook tips.

The project was very well received. The managers were proud of talking about their teams, projects, and accomplishments. The participants gave positive feedback informing that they could now understand better the products we were delivering and how each one of us was adding value to the business. When I left the company, a colleague told me that she wanted to be responsible for the activity to keep up the good work initiated by me.

The main outcomes of this initiative were increase in collaboration, pride, effectiveness and productivity. In addition, it was indirectly contributing to a happier and more agile workplace.

What do you need to have an agile career strategy? Check the list below and define the areas that need improvement. Create an action plan to start implementing new agile habits into your operational day-to-day.

Action	Purpose	Who can help you?	What do you need to get the action done quicker?

Remember that your career is a mosaic of opportunities that are building your professional future. Planners tend to think that strategy is a blueprint, a book, or a product that is finished and fixed once it is done. But strategy does not deserve the name unless it is evolutionary and highly adaptive. So, be strategically agile!

As the author and leadership expert Thomas D. Zweifel states, "Strategy is a moving target, it must constantly change in response to the new landscape given by action, and it must be systematically and regularly challenged to stay relevant."

HAVING AN AGILE CAREER STRATEGY WILL HELP YOU:

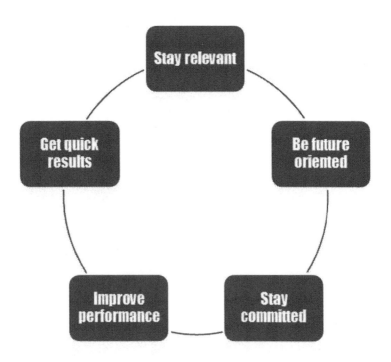

Thinking sustainability

When we think sustainability, we see towards the future with the tools we have in the present. The meaning of sustainability in the dictionary refers to something that is able to continue over a period of time. Some other words related to sustainability are durable, enduring, lasting, strong, prolonged, and established.

A sustainable career is one which will allow you to perform interesting work that exploits all your talents, still offering you opportunities for growth while also increasing the value you provide to your company. A lasting career is a journey in continuous improving mode.

As Monique Valcour, an executive coach, keynote speaker, and management professor writes in her article 'Craft a Sustainable Career', "a sustainable career is dynamic and flexible; it features continuous learning, periodic renewal, the security that comes from employability, and a harmonious fit with your skills, interests, and values." The five strategies to build a strong and durable career path adapted from the article are related to topics already presented in this book.

THE FIVE STRATEGIES FOR A SUSTAINABLE CAREER

1	Take ownership for your career development
2	Constantly assess and identify how to keep adding value to your employer
3	Connect your achievements to your career goals
4	Follow the developments and trends in your industry and the strategic course of your company
5	Surround yourself with people who energize you

I suggest that you work through the topics in Chapter Three "Aligning the Goals", to ensure that you understand how to practice the strategies one to four (from the list above) in your day-to-day at work by creating synergy, becoming a strategic enabler, and being committed to learning.

For strategy five (from the list above), there is detailed advice earlier in this chapter about building a strategic network and being surrounded by people who can bring enthusiasm and energy to the process. Because people are the most important thing in executing strategies.

A sustainable career is built upon the ability to show that you can fill a need that someone is willing to pay for.
—Monique Valcour

ACTION ITEMS

1. Go back to the topic "What is an agile mindset?" in this chapter and choose three activities that you want to incorporate to your career strategy that will help you execute your plan in an agile way.
2. Link the activities to SMART goals.

5

Achieving Success

However beautiful the strategy, you should occasionally look at the results.
–Sir Winston Churchill

Strategy planning is a process, not an event. To succeed, we have to keep evaluating the process. Keep being curious. Keep eliminating orthodoxies and questioning the status quo.

"There are always two parties, the party of the past and the party of the future; the establishment and the movement" wrote Ralph Emerson.

Be a defender of better future!

- What is working well?

- What can I do better?

- Am I engaged enough?

- Do I need more information to be committed enough?

- What is missing?

- What are the blockages?

- And what are the opportunities?

You have to keep asking these questions during the whole process.

You also need to have in mind the "why" of having a strategy. It will empower you.

We need a strategy because we need to know the why of what we are doing, to follow the right paths to achieve our dreams and goals, understand the importance of our work in the grand schemed of things, structure the tasks we are performing, keep growing, ensure competitive advantage and enhance engagement.

People thrive when they have a purpose! It is wonderful that a job can provide an income and a standard of living, but isn't there something more than that?

We need to keep in mind that if we do not consciously develop ourselves on an ongoing basis throughout our careers, we will slowly become irrelevant. Staying relevant is the biggest threat we face as professionals.

Build in the time in your schedule for revising your strategy, actions plan, goals, dreams, passion, vision and professional purpose. This is key for success. As we will be learning new things along the way, we will also need to reformulate our plans and find new directions to follow.

The success of your strategy career plan is about keeping on identifying where you want to be in the future. Go after what you want; even if you believe you are not quite ready.

You are the CEO of your career! Right?

Reflection takes time and effort

My intention in writing this book is not to present new concepts, ideas or revolutionary thoughts. I want this book to be your reflection-time, your strategic thinking moment and a source of inspiration to your self-assessments.

Regular self-assessments will increase the possibilities for doing good both for yourself and others.
– Julia Schmidt

Reflection is an important way to change and develop, by looking back and thinking about what you have done, how you can apply the things you have learned, and defining what you need to keep on achieving your goals. Avoid acting on autopilot mode! It is an active choice to stop and reflect. Listen to others as well as to yourself.

• What do people have to say that I can learn from?

- Do I schedule time for strategic thinking?

- Do I find time during the week to evaluate my goals and failures?

- Do I have a mentor who helps me go in reflection mode?

- Do I ask myself what has been my biggest success or major challenge?

- What are I committed to achieve in the next seven days?

- What help do I need now?

To succeed in your career planning, you have to make reflection a new habit. It will lead you to constructive evaluation processes. You have to learn from what works and, significantly, from what does not work.

A successful career is not something ready-made. It comes from daily actions, decisions and your own hard work.
– Julia Schmidt

A successful career journey is about being open to a lifelong learning journey. What we will learn on the way is crucial for making necessary adjustments, improvements and changes that will insure effective and desired results. What we learn is what will bring us further and do things better today than what we did yesterday. Success for me is clearly linked to everything I learn and apply to my life and work.

Assessment is an integral part of learning processes, and any career journey has a set of learning processes. Assessment affects decisions, choices, and results.

A positive outcome of achieved accomplishments

Accomplishment is often associated with success, but it is not the same.

Keep in mind that success is the consequence of having earned a series of accomplishments. So they are part of a process that will lead you towards wealth and a journey full of success.

Understanding the overall definitions of failure, accomplishment and success from a dictionary may help us in defining our own meaning for career success.

Failure is a lack of success in doing or achieving something, especially in relation to a particular activity.

An **achievement** is something which someone has succeeded in doing, especially after a lot of effort. It is the process of achieving something or attaining a goal.

Success is the achievement of something that you have been trying to do. It is a favorable outcome of something attempted. The success of something is the fact that it works in a satisfactory way or has the result that is intended.

The dictionary also describes success as the following: fortune, prosperity, riches, lucky.

Success quotes

The use of quotes is very useful in supporting our thoughts and opening our mind to new perspectives of seeing different aspects of life. Quotes help me open up my creativity and lateral thinking. Many quotes about success remind us that success is a positive outcome that is close related to effort, learning, goal setting, actions and improvement. In the following, I have found some very inspiring and motivating quotes that shall support you on your career journey.

There are no secrets to success. It is the result of preparation, hard work, and learning from failure.
— Colin Powell

Success seems to be connected with action. Successful people keep moving. They make mistakes, but they don't quit.
— Conrad Hilton

I never dreamed about success, I worked for it.
— Estee Lauder

Without continual growth and progress, such words as improvement, achievement, and success have no meaning.
— Benjamin Franklin

Think little goals and expect little achievements. Think big goals and win big success.
— David Joseph Schwartz

Success is not a destination, but the road that you're on. Being successful means that you're working hard and walking your walk every day. You can only live your dream by working hard towards it. That's living your dream.
— Marlon Wayans

The quotes above tell us about crucial elements in achieving success in our career, and embracing it as a process, not a destination.

Key elements for achieving success

Define your own success! It can be associated with happiness, living up to your potential, enjoying life, wealth, writing a symphony, becoming an entrepreneur, or just becoming the best professional you can be. **Career success means different things to different people.**

The intention of this book is not to share any formulas. I want you to stop, reflect and create your own career strategy. Pick up what you think will work for you.

Here are some of the key elements I have identified during my career journey and inspired by some readings about the topic. These are my key elements, you can elaborate your own essentials and make the list that will support you in achieving your success moments.

Listen – Actively listening to team members, co-workers, advisors and mentors will help you have different perspectives.

Be organized – There is so much information you need to work with in order to form your strategy and create the actions that will help you attain your goals.

Be curious – Read the great books, master as many skills as possible, learn something new every day, and redefine your strategy whenever necessary.

Be committed – Knowing why you are on your career road and doing everything you can to keep on the good direction will give you drive. Staying committed is about dedication, discipline, optimism and positive thoughts. As the 14th and current Dalai Lama, Tenzin Gyatso, notes, "Just one small positive thought in the morning can change your whole day." So, can you imagine how big a difference it can make in your whole career life?

Be resilient – Being resilient is all about practicing flexibility, tolerance and positive thinking. I usually study the different ways to attain my goals by thinking: "I want to attain this goal well and for that I need to …" The best way to avoid stress, high frustration, uncertainty and fear is by seeing the big picture, being prepared and avoiding procrastination.

Know what not to do – In executing your strategy plan you will face a lot of things that need to be handled properly. If you try to focus on too much you will scatter your energy and lose your effectiveness. To succeed, sort out major issues from minor ones. Selectively disengage from some strategic activities so that you can powerfully engage in the most relevant. Assess how you are spending time and energy as often as possible.

Take care of you – The pursuit of your goals, success and accomplishments demands hard work, dedication, time and extraordinary effort and focus. Therefore, you must understand that "there is virtue in work and there is virtue in rest," as said by Alan Cohen, author of many inspirational books. So, take time for yourself each day and for what helps you charge your batteries. My website on Facebook called Organizational Health and Wellbeing for Assistants works as a kind of wellbeing reminder.

Don't forget your family – A job is just a job. If you marry your job from the beginning of your career, prepare to be alone when you retire. Take your family with you in your career journey. Do not abandon them. We need people! We need the best people we can have with us in this. Knowing the Why is about being able to view and understand the big picture. The Why will help us think and act strategically.

Juggle your expectations and deadlines – Your career journey is a long trip with many incidents, detours, roadblocks, potholes, and surprises. Some beautiful paths during our career journey cannot be discovered without getting lost, finding new ways, creating new expectations and embracing flexibility. I believe that any career success is about juggling with expectations and deadlines in a structured and resilient way. So read the topics in this part about accepting failure, knowing what to do, being resilient, being accountable, keeping a log of activities, being realist, being organized, staying focused, and taking care of you. They will help you solve the puzzle.

Follow your core values – They are what support your vision, shape your behaviour, and reflect your personal and professional standards. They are your principles and beliefs. As we learned in Chapter Two, your values will help you create your purpose. In your career journey, every time you notice that what you are doing is not reflecting what you stand for or believe, then you have to go back to Chapter Two in this book and re-do the exercises and self-assessments. Your values are the tool-set which will open doors for your success moments.

Accept the possibility of failure – There is no success without failure. So, the main question you must ask yourself every day is "What can I learn from my failures?" We fail in order to grow. Without ever failing, we would never progress in our goals.

Be an enabler – A common personality trait of an enabler is to be helpful. By empowering others, you will be enabling positive behavior in yourself which will allow growth and development.

Keep a log of activities – To accomplish your long-term goals you have to make continuous progress on a day-to-day basis. To ensure that you move towards your goals, day after day, keep a log with all specific tasks you need to accomplish every day. Create an objective for each day and list the tasks accordingly. For each day ask yourself "How are today's tasks bringing me closer to my long-term goals?"

Be accountable – In the workplace, the employee accountability is the responsibility to complete the tasks that are assigned, perform the duties required by the job, and to be ready to fulfill any new activities to help the organization attain its goals. In planning and executing your career strategy, the same is required. What you need is to follow your mission, set and follow your career goals, create your activity log, do one task at a time, emphasize your strengths, value your time, evaluate your performance, embrace feedback as a gift, and reward yourself.

Stay focused – Have a plan and follow your activity log, know the objective for the day and work to complete it without distractions. Give yourself time to rest and recover your batteries. If social media use is preventing you from dedicating the right time to fulfill your goals, eliminate it from your operational day. Owning your time and administrating it will help you create a focus workspace for your career. The single greatest obstacle to being focused in this digital age is your technology, including computers, tablets, and smartphones. I have no pings, vibrations, and other notifications signaling to me that a voicemail, email, text message, or social media update has arrived to me. It gives me at least 50% control of my time. It is also helping me write this book and deliver it in time to my editor.

Know your Why – As we learned in the first chapter of this book, we need a strategy because we need to know the why of what we are doing, to follow the right paths to achieve our dreams and goals, understand the importance of our work in the grand scheme of things, structure the tasks we are performing, ensure competitive advantage, keep growing, and enhance engagement. Knowing the Why is about being able to view and understand the big picture, and think and act strategically in a consistent way.

Be a realist – No one knows you better then yourself. Break your strategy plan into realistic tasks, manageable pieces and set solid deadlines for achieving them. Do not let failure take you out of the road. Once you have all your ducks in a row, take a deep breath and dive in. Move! Take action!

What successful moments did you have in your career?

I want you to identify some of the successful moments you have experienced in private and professional life. You must have in mind that your career is a journey that embraces both personal and professional sides. List 10 moments for each topic.

Column A: Private life	Column B: Professional life
1a	1b
2a	2b
3a	3b
4a	4b
5a	5b
6a	6b
7a	7b
8a	8b
9a	9b
10a	10b

Now, I want you to choose three successful moments from your professional life column and write them down here below.

My preferred career success moments
1
2
3

In the next exercise, I want you to assess your three preferred success moments and link them to accomplishments.

In column 1, you will write your three preferred career success moments and in column 2, you will write the accomplishments that led to each success moment. You can read the example from my career to help you understand how to start filling in the table.

Suppose that one of my preferred success moments is when I got promoted from Executive Assistant to Senior Executive Assistant. So that is what I am going to write in column #1: Promotion from EA to senior EA in 2018. In column #2, I will write the accomplishments related to the promotion, which are first, increased company knowledge, second, good results in improving the company's internal communication, and third, successful onboarding of the new CEO.

Column 1 My preferred success moments from my professional life (Write the three preferred success moments from the previous exercise in this column)	Column 2 Which accomplishments were related to these outcomes? (List 1 to 3 accomplishments that helped you attain the success moment listed in column 1)
1	1. 2. 3.

2	1.
	2.
	3.
3	1.
	2.
	3.

Now think about your feelings when you experienced your great success moments.

Did these moments give you motivation?

Where they related to specific career goals?

Did they make you feel proud of your job and career?

What did this exercise tell you about

- your true source of motivation,

- being prepared,

- embracing hard work, and

- setting goals?

How can you make these success moments happen again?

I suggest that you do this exercise two to three times a year. It will be like giving yourself a performance review.

What does success mean for you?

Career success means different things to different people. Now is the time for you to create your own success definition.
Inspired by what you have read in this chapter and your success moments, write your success definition here.

MY OWN SUCCESS DEFINITION

ACTION ITEMS

1. Go to one of the many "quote creator" sites and transform your meaningful success definition into a beautiful quote poster.
2. If you are a fan of social media, choose your preferred channel and post your success quote there. Share it with friends and colleagues.

6

Inspirational Quotes on Strategy Execution

1. "Strategy is no longer chiseled in stone; it has become as flexible and changeable as life itself."

   – Laura Stack, writer and expert in employee and team productivity.

2. "Strategy is not a solo sport, even if you're the CEO."

   – Max McKeown, an English writer, consultant, and researcher specializing in innovation strategy, leadership and culture.

3. "Individually, we are one drop. Together, we are an ocean."

   – Ryunosuke Satoro, a Japanese writer.

4. "There has never been a greater need for good strategy and execution than today." "Strategy execution is the responsibility that makes or breaks executives."

– Alan Brache and Sam Bodley-Scott, authors of the book 'Implementation: How to Transform Strategic Initiatives into Blockbuster Results'.

5. "Execution is a specific set of behaviours and techniques that companies need to master in order to have competitive advantage. It's a discipline of its own."

– Ram Charan and Larry Bossidy, authors of the book 'Execution: The Discipline of Getting Things Done'.

6. "The essence of strategy is choosing what not to do."

– Michael E. Porter, an economist, researcher, author, advisor, speaker and teacher.

7. "Strategy without tactics is the slowest route to victory. Tactics without strategy is the noise before defeat."

– Sun Tzu, a Chinese general, military strategist, writer and philosopher.

8. "There is nothing so useless as doing efficiently that which should not be done at all."

– Peter Drucker, a management consultant, educator, and author.

9. "The real challenge in crafting strategy lies in detecting subtle discontinuities that may undermine a business in the future. And for that there is no technique, no program, just a sharp mind in touch with the situation."

– Henry Mintzberg, Canadian academic and author on business and management.

10. "In McKinsey's world, all of life is one of two things: strategy or organization."

– Tom Peters, writer on business management practices and former management consultant at McKinsey & Company.

11. "In real life, strategy is actually very straightforward. You pick a general direction and implement like hell."

– Jack Welch, former GE CEO.

12. "What's the use of running if you are not on the right road?

– German proverb.

13. "The result of bad communication is a disconnection between strategy and execution."

– Chuck Martin, former vice president, IBM.

14. "Rather than a business plan or a book or a document, a good strategy provides openings for action – in other words, irresistible opportunities for decisive moves – and a freedom to be; in other words, it unfetters people's leadership, creativity, and innovation."

– Thomas D. Zweifel, author and leadership expert.

Reading Recommendations

This list includes some of the important books I have read to give me support in building a powerful and sustainable career, and more.

The 7 Habits of Highly Effective People by Stephen R. Covey – because all successful executive assistants need to be prepared to become a better leader.

The Business Strategy Toolkit by David Cotton – because strategy is much more than sexy stuff; it is the cornerstone of success.

TED Talks – The Official TED Guide to Public Speaking – because public speaking is a necessary leadership skill to inspire people and enable knowledge sharing and growth.

The First 90 Days – Proven Strategies for Getting Up to Speed Faster and Smarter by Michael D. Watkins – because moving to a new role is always a big challenge for a professional to face.

The Future of Work – Attract New Talent, Build Better Leaders, and Create a Competitive Organization by Jacob Morgan – because in building our career strategy we need to understand what is next for the workplace in the future of work.

Reinventing Work: The Brand You 50 by Tom Peters – because your career strategy is about YOU and you are what you do.

What Color Is Your Parachute? 2019: A Practical Manual For Job-Hunters And Career-Changers by Richard N. Bolles – because we all need from time to time to evaluate our choices and take new directions.

Agile People: A Radical Approach For HR & Managers (That Leads To Motivated Employees) by Pia-Maria Thoren – because employee priorities are changing and we need to ensure our motivation, step out of our comfort zones and adapt to younger, newer ways of thinking.

Where will you be five years from today? by Dan Zadra – because we need to decide what's next in our life and strategise how to get it.

Work Your Package: A Guide To Being The Total Package by Ayanna Castro – because our talents are the most important assets in our career journey.

Act Like A Leader, Think Like A Leader by Hermina Ibarra – because strategic thinking comes from believing that we can "transform by doing."

"Today a reader, tomorrow a leader."
– Margaret Fuller

Final Words

These aren't any final words. The final words are the ones you will choose yourself and own. In fact, this is just the beginning.
– Julia Schmidt

The best day of your career journey is the one on which you decide that your professional career is your own, and that you can have as many people as you want in this journey with you.

I hope you are going to do great things with everything you have read in this book.

Start your journey now! Your journey is determined by your choices.

Get on the road again, if you feel lost. It is never too late to become the CEO of your career. Remember that it is YOUR journey, decisions, actions, assessments and learning. All adversity will help you learn, find new solutions, take new paths, stop and use time to reflect and check your roadmap. It will not take a few days or years. The journey will not bring you from one place to another one, but many times to more than one place – also to unexpected places. Your career trip is your life road – it is a long distance and often in challenging circumstances. It is no ordinary trip. It is your unique life.

Owning your career journey is about identifying your performance criteria, understanding what to do to attain the expected outcomes and making the right decisions. I want you to know where you are going and to find the best roads to take you there, where you see your success.

Thank you for joining me on this journey! I wish you a successful and sustainable career!

If you found this book helpful or inspiring in any way, I hope you will take a moment to write a short review. Your feedback is greatly appreciated.

Please also consider joining me on LinkedIn to keep up to date with me and share your views about the book.

Acknowledgments

I would like to thank those who have been part of my career trip. They are my family, friends, peers from IMA – International Management Assistant – colleagues and role models.

Special thanks to the Executive Secretary Magazine team, and specially to Lucy Brazier, CEO of Marcham Publishing, Matthew Want, Executive Assistant to the CEO, and Kathleen Drum, Senior Editor of Executive Secretary Magazine – you have helped me understand that I am part of a family that enables growth, professionalism and enthusiasm. Thank you for having given me space to express my ideas and share knowledge through my articles – the pillars of this book. It was first a promise, then a goal expressed during my interview by Kathleen Drum in 2017 when my answer to the question about my plans for the future was "In five years time, I want to have published my first book."

This dream could not have become a reality without the support of all my readers, proofreaders and co-writers during the past five years, some of them are Alan Newton, Paula Moio, Nico Jones, Jennifer Corcoran, Angela Parker, Chiara Agnese Azzarello, Claire Grace, Else-Britt Lundgren, Sofie Koark, Jaqueline F. Svensson, Kristin Sandvik, Helen Monument, Kemetia Foley, Andrea Macarie, Carla Stefanut, Diana Brandl, and Bonnie Low-Kramen. You were empowering me with your feedback, encouragement, and co-writing partnership.

I am profoundly grateful to my friend Nora Nordan, who read the introduction to the book. I am thankful for your suggestions – and corrections – as well as for the incredible support in making me believe that this book would be an enjoyable reading for many administrative professionals.

Thank you to my editor Alistair Lowde for proofreading, copy-editing, design and book layout, Kindle book creation and book publication. Also, for motivating me to work during my weekends and being an expert friend along the way.

To my parents, Marina and Ranulfo, you literally did everything you could to give your children the best education. Thank you for being the best parents in the world.

About the Author

Julia Schmidt has worked as an Executive Assistant for over 25 years, holding roles in Brazil, her home country, and Norway, where she has been living since 1998. She has worked in industries as different as Public sector, Bank and Finance, Publishing, Oil & Gas services, and IT. Julia has written many articles to the Executive Secretary Magazine and blogs about Organizational Health and Wellbeing, Leadership and Career Development.

Julia is an active networker, public speaker, mentor and past National Chairman (2016-2018) of IMA Norway – International Management Assistants, with a passion for people development and helping others embrace their leadership skills. She created the hashtag #BeTheBestAssistant to spread her commitment to excel.

She is a proud graduate of the University of Norway with a Masters' Degree in Portuguese Language and Literature and has certifications in Business Administration.

In 2017, she was awarded PA of The Year Scandinavia. In 2018, she represented Norway at the 10th World Administrator's Summit in Frankfurt, Germany, hosted by IMA.

Index

Printed in Great Britain
by Amazon